I0459876

The Elders' Book
of Cherishing

The Elders' Book of Cherishing

of Cherishing

Coming Back to the Vision at the Beginning
of the Lord's Recovery

STEPHEN ISITT

ARPress
ILLUMINATING IDEAS.
EMPOWERING VOICES

Copyright © 2025 by Stephen Isitt

All rights reserved. No part of this publication may be reproduced, distributed, or transmitted in any form or by any means, including photocopying, recording, or other electronic or mechanical methods, without the prior written permission of the copyright owner and the publisher, except in the case of brief quotations embodied in critical reviews and certain other noncommercial uses permitted by copyright law.For permission requests,write to the publisher, addressed "Attention: Permissions Coordinator," at the address below.

ARPress
45 Dan Road Suite 5
Canton, MA 02021

Hotline: 1(888) 821-0229
Fax: 1(508) 545-7580

Ordering Information:
Quantity sales. Special discounts are available on quantity purchases by corporations,associations, and others. For details, contact the publisher at the address above.

Printed in the United States of America.

ISBN-13:   Softcover   979-8-89676-282-9
              eBook   979-8-89676-283-6

Library of Congress Control Number: 2025907042

The Elders' Book
of Cherishing

I Thess. 2:7

But we were gentle in your midst, as a nursing mother would cherish (tenderly care for) her own children.

***

Cherishing, which includes nourishing, indicates care that is more tender than mere nourishing. – Witness Lee (I Thess. 2:7 Recovery Version footnote)

***

The condition of a church depends upon the eldership in that church. The proper eldership is one in which all the elders contact people daily, weekly, regularly, and consistently. The number of people the elders contact is the deciding factor of the condition of the church in their locality. - Witness Lee, 1991, Elders' Training Book 11, p. 20

Table of Contents

Bearing Burdens

"**Brothers, if you do not learn how to bear the burdens of others, and if you do not seek out the help from others regarding your own burdens, you do not know what the Body is, nor can you have coordination in the work...**If we stay in our former condition, we are still tightly wrapped in ourselves... Then my affairs are still my affairs, and I will not let you touch them... When problems come, you have never once sought someone saying 'I need help'. We need to be an open person...Toward your brother your spirit needs to be open, your thinking needs to be open, and many times your mouth needs to be opened. **I hope there will be those among us who can say to the brothers and sisters, 'I have had trouble with this one matter for many years. Please help me overcome it.' If this is the first time in your life that you ask for help, let it be here [on the mountain]**" (p.179-181, Church Affairs, W. Nee)

1

Touching the Soul

"In the past we may have thought that we need to shepherd people's spirits. We stress the spirit of man, and we tell people to reject the soul. But we need to realize that the saints' problems are with their soul. We may feel that if their spirit is strong, there will be no problem. But how could their spirit be strong when they have a lot of problems in their soul. Thus, we need to learn how to shepherd their souls, how to touch their soul. Today on this earth, there is not one person who does not have any problem in his soul. This is why I encourage you all to open up yourself to your fellow brothers so that the Lord can have a way to shepherd your soul. We need this kind of shepherding" (The Training and Practice of VG, p.77, W. Lee).

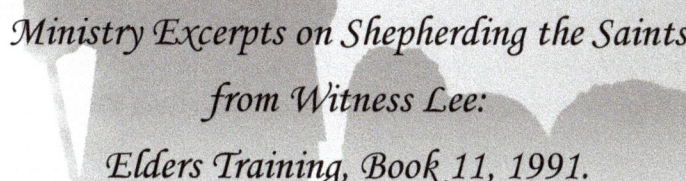

Ministry Excerpts on Shepherding the Saints
from Witness Lee:
Elders Training, Book 11, 1991.

1. **"The condition of a church depends upon the eldership in that church. The proper eldership is one in which all the elders contact people daily, weekly, regularly, and consistently. The number of people the elders contact is the deciding factor of the condition of the church in their locality."**

2. *"We must first pick up a concern for people and go to contact them. Then we will learn their condition."*

3. *"They need to go to each of the saints' homes outside [the meetings of the church]. This is why Paul said in Acts 20 that he taught the saints publicly and from house to house and that he admonished each one of them night and day with tears. Paul used both the day and the night."*

4. *"We mostly use the meeting time to contact the saints. We think that as long as we have attended every meeting, we have fulfilled our duty. But that is not the complete fulfilling of our duty. The fulfilling of our duty is also outside the meetings."*

5. **"…The elders must pick up the burden of a slave to serve the big family of their Master."**

6. *"Paul did not withdraw from his responsibility. Rather, he taught the believers publicly in the meetings and privately from house to house."*

7. *"From now on the elders should do more home visitation. By visiting the homes of the saints, the elders can teach and shepherd the saints."*

8. **"To shepherd is not just to give a message. This is neither adequate nor primary. The primary responsibility is to go to the saints and shepherd them in their homes. So Paul set up a pattern for the elders by teaching the saints publicly and from house to house. If there is a house, the elders should go. If there are ten houses, they should go to each one to visit each of the saints."**

9. *"By visiting a home, the real situation of that person's environment could be seen. Then the elders could render them the proper shepherding."*

10. *"Although we need to mow the lawn, keep our house clean and neat, clean the windows, and vacuum the carpet, do not spend that much time on these things. Rather, we should save some of the time to shepherd the saints.* **If we go to the homes of the saints to shepherd them, there will be a record of this in the heavens."**

11. *"In Acts 20:27 Paul continues to say, 'For I did not shrink from declaring to you all the counsel of God'. Not only did Paul teach them, care for their interests, and care for the things that were profitable to them, but he declared also God's counsel, God's plan, and God's economy."*

12. *"In verse 28, Paul admonishes the elders to 'take heed to yourselves and to all the flock, among whom the Holy Spirit has placed you as overseers'."*

13. **"An overseer should not be sloppy or sleepy but all the time watchful. He must be aware of the situation of the church, and oversee each member of the flock. If so, he will know what the need is and what they should do."**

14. *"Our lack is in the actual practice of the God-ordained way. According to the actual practice, the God-ordained way replaces the papal system and the clergy-laity system. This practice altogether depends upon the functioning of all the members of the Body of Christ to contact people individually, one by one."*

15. *"We should not despise the individual contact with people. As long as we do not practice the New Testament priesthood of the gospel by contacting people, one by one, we are still somewhat remaining in the papal and clergy-laity systems."*

16. ***"It is easier to practice the old, organizational clergy-laity system than it is to gain people one by one and present them as sacrifices to God."***

17. *"…We need the individual, direct contact with people, one on one… This requires much endeavor and labor. Instead of doing this, though, many of us are occupied with other things that we think are necessary. For the managing of the church, these things may be right, but actually they are not so necessary.* ***For the managing of the church in their locality the necessary thing for the elders is to visit people and contact them one by one."***

18. *"We have to endeavor to pick up our 'fork' and throw away the 'chopsticks'. To pick up the fork is to pick up the practice of contacting people one by one. This is why I have said that the elders should endeavor to contact twenty people a week.* ***Contacting people one by one saves us from building up a religion. This personal contact with people builds up the Body of Christ. This is a very serious matter.***

"Paul charged the elders not only to teach but to shepherd the church of God which God obtained through His own blood. To obtain also denotes to acquire, or purchase. His own blood is a dear term. God considers the church as a treasure, which is very dear and precious in His eyes. He loves the church to such an extent that He purchased it with His own blood."

"Similarly, the elders should also love the church as God does. Even the parents always save the best things for their dear children. God used His own blood. So we must love the church with this kind of fine feeling and affection."

20. *"Finally, verse 31 says, 'Wherefore watch, remembering that for three years, night and day, I did not cease admonishing each one with tears.' Paul did not only go to their house, but he also admonished each one of them with tears day and night. The elders among us must learn to pick up a burden to do this day and night. They should go to the homes of the saints and admonish each one with tears."*

21. *"…At times rebuking and advising may not do as much good as dropping your tears."*

22. *"Paul was a very emotional person. Acts 20 mentions tears twice. In verse 19, Paul served the Lord with humility, tears and trials. Again, in verse 31, he spent three years, night and day, admonishing each one with tears. This kind of admonishing is the necessary responsibility of the elders."*

23. ***"The necessary thing for the elders is to visit people and contact them one by one."***

A Timely Trumpeting and The Present Need
(W. L., 1988, excerpts from the book)

24. *"First Peter 5:1-2 says, '…the elders…shepherd the flock of God'. This shows us that the church is the flock of God. It is entrusted to the shepherding of the elders. An elder is a shepherd. **He cannot care for the sheep according to his mood, enthusiastic today, negligent tomorrow. The care for the flock is a daily matter.** We have to care for the flock daily and unceasingly, until the Chief Shepherd is manifested (I Pet. 5:4). This means that there is no end to the care for the saints. We do not know on what day the Lord will come. We only know to labor in care for the flock. If we do not have this spirit, it will be impossible for any of us to be a co-worker or an elder."*

25. **"In order to take care of the church properly, the elders have to take this charge from the Lord. They must shepherd the saints conscientiously."**

26. *"To shepherd the saints is to take care of all the needs of the sheep."*

27. **"[The elders] should do their best to shepherd and care for the saints. As soon as we hear of anyone sick or of anyone encountering problems, we must be concerned for him, pray for him, and go to visit him. The impact that this little bit of concern, prayer, and visiting affords is far more powerful than ten messages."**

28. **"Care can touch people's feeling in a far deeper way than messages can."**

29. **"...The elders must have the compassion of a caring mother. They must be desperate to care for the Lord's lambs."**

30. *"If the elders and co-workers would love the saints like a mother who loves her child and would render a loving, willing service to them... every one of them will be able to do the work that the co-workers and elders do."*

An Elders' Conference on Shepherding
1998 (WL quotes based on material used)

31. **"The first responsibility of an elder is to always have an interest and concern for others' spiritual welfare."**

32. *"When the elders are very involved with the church's business affairs, the church does not have a promising future. It is better that the elders spend most of their time to contact people."*

33. *"It is better that their heart not be in the [business] affairs but on people."*

34. **"They should be concerned for people, have an interest in people, and be fully occupied with people."**

35. *"The elders should pick up the habit to care for people and seek the help of others for the business affairs."*

36. **"The elders must also learn to contact people. According to my observation and experience, an elder should contact about one hundred persons a month. This means he would contact about 3-4 persons daily."**

37. *"Many of the elders are not full-timers. Therefore, they must budget their time to contact people each day. An elder in a local church must budget his time to contact at least two people each day."*

38. *"The elders should contact all kinds of people, including unbelievers, new believers, and weak believers."*

39. *"The elders must pick up a burden to contact people in this way and to assign all the business affairs to the serving ones. This will save the elders from the business of the church so that they can care for people."*

40. *"The interest in others' spiritual welfare is the interest concerning people's condition with the Lord, which ministers life in the organic building up of the Body of Christ. We cannot know people's condition with the Lord except by direct contact with them."*

41. **"No one can know someone's real condition unless he contacts him a number of times."**

> **"We must contact someone again and again, until he has a trust in us and will open up the things on his heart. Without this, we cannot know his real condition."**

43. *"The elders must be burdened with the contacting of people for the Lord's kingdom. It is not sufficient merely to be concerned for people. The elders must pick up the burden to contact people."*

44. *"When the elders go to contact people, or when people come to contact them, they must always open themselves up in order to gain the credit of the ones they contact."*

45. *"The contact we have with people is always based upon our opening to them"* [with wisdom].

46. *"The elders must also learn to pray with a particular burden for the relationship with the Lord of those for whom they are concerned."*

47. *"If the elders take the way we have fellowshipped here, they will be very approachable. It will be easy for people to contact them."*

48. *"All the elders should learn to contact people. The elders should save their time from meaningless telephone calls and conversations.* **We must change our way of living.***"*

49. *"The elders should schedule their time in a very narrow and strict way. In this way, they can fulfill their responsibility in the eldership.* **Without contacting people, they will have no way to fulfill their responsibility.***"*

50. **"The condition of a church depends upon the eldership in that church. The proper eldership is one in which all the elders contact people daily, weekly, regularly, and consistently. The number of people the elders contact is the deciding factor of the condition of the church in their locality."**

51. *"We must pick up a concern for people and go to contact them. Then we will learn their condition."*

52. *"In a local church the first thing that is needed is for the elders to contact people. It is very convenient, profitable, and necessary for them to contact*

11

people…before and after the meetings. However, many elders have not picked up this habit."

53. **"The elders should contact two or three persons a day. Whether or not this is difficult for us depends on our habit. We may not have practiced and exercised to contact people until it has become our habit."**

54. *"Moreover, we may not have been born as persons who like to contact people. However, in the ministry we are compelled, forced, to forget about ourselves and contact people."*

55. *"The elders need to be adjusted in the matter of contacting people in a successful way. They must answer to the Lord regarding how many persons have been brought to the Lord through them since they became elders and whether their way to contact people is more effective today then it was five years ago."*

56. *"An elder should be concerned about whether or not he has contacted people in an adequate way."*

57. **"It is a failure for an elder not to contact people for several days. All the people in the church need the care of the elders."**

58. **"The elders can only render care by contacting them."**

59. *"In their contact with people, the elders should minister Christ to them to meet their need" (Eph. 3:8; Col. 1:28).*

60. *"They should minister Christ to everyone — stronger ones and weaker ones, the overcoming ones and the defeated ones, those with good background and those with a bad background."*

61. *"We must be the same toward every person. It is easy for us to minister life to a brother we regard highly, but we may be cold and indifferent toward another kind of brother."*

62. *"In the matter of ministering Christ to others, we may still have our own choice and preference."*

63. *"We may be willing to contact a brother like Timothy, but we may not take the time to help a brother like Demas, who loved the world and forsook Paul."*

64. *"We may welcome Timothy but despise and reject Demas because Demas had a failure."*

65. ***"Many of us like to help the good ones, but it seems that we feel the undesirable ones are destined to be lost. No one seems to care for them."***

66. *"If we only care for the good ones, it is no wonder that the church does not have the increase."*

67. *"The Lord Jesus was zealous in contacting the bad person [like Zaccheus]. The elders should learn how to help the ones who are not good."*

68. *"If we learn that certain persons are not good and as a result do not care for them, we lose the opportunity to minister Christ to them."*

69. *"Every member of the Body is indispensable (I Cor. 12:22). Do we really believe that every member of the Body in our local church is needed? We may say this, but we do not practice it."*

70. ***"We actually think that some of the saints are not that important. Whether they are among us or not, we feel about the same. But Paul said that even the weakest ones, the smallest ones, are needed in the Body of Christ."***

71. *"Paul said that the less honorable members of the Body are clothed with more abundant honor, and the uncomely members are given more abundant comeliness; but the comely members have no need. According to Paul, God adorns only the less honorable and the comely ones."*

72. *"We may feel that the one who is not smart is useless and that the Body does not need him. But the Body of Christ needs all the members because every member is indispensable."*

73. **"We should not evaluate anyone, but we need to have the same care for one another."**

74. *"Regardless of what we see or hear about others, we should not forget what our responsibility is...to minister Christ to them."*

75. *"We should not care much for others' position and condition. Regardless of their condition, we should still minister Christ to them with Christ's salvation."*

76. *"When we contact people, we should not care for what we see about them or hear about them. We must take care of our business to minister Christ with His salvation. Whether someone is a 'Zaccheus' or an 'immoral woman of Samaria', we should do the same thing."*

77. *"Suppose a backslidden brother comes to us. If we still remember and are deeply impressed with his backsliding, this remembrance will reduce our usefulness in the hand of the Lord. We should forget about his backsliding. He is still a brother, and our duty, our business, in the eldership is to minister Christ to him."*

78. **"We should love everyone on the same level of love. We should care for all the saints though some may not like us."**

79. *"Nearly all the elders, full-timers, and co-workers serve people according to their choice, their preference, and their evaluation."*

80. *"When a certain one invites us to their home we will go because they are our favorite. If another one invites us, we will refuse, excusing ourselves because we are too busy or too tired."*

81. *"Our evaluation of others frustrates us. Our natural sight kills us."*

> *"In the flesh everybody is nothing. In Christ, we all are the new creation. Therefore, we should not evaluate people. We should just learn to minister Christ to others. We minister Christ to someone to build up the new creation within him."*

83. *"We should not trust our evaluation of others. We should simply minister Christ to build them up."*

84. *"In their contact with people, the elders should seek a way to get people to open to them. We must find a way to create a hunger for the Lord within them."*

85. *"If we would practice to always seek a way to get people to open to us, to find the proper utterance to touch people's spirit, to catch the proper time to dispense Christ either by a verse or by our inspiration, and to know how to create an appetite to cause people to hunger and thirst after the Lord,* **the attendance of the church meetings will be increased."**

86. *"We must change our way of contacting people, staying away from catching or condemning people, and learning to minister Christ to every kind of person. Eventually, people will be gained by the Lord through our contact."*

87. *"I have rarely seen a place where the elders promoted, adjusted, and improved the spirit, attitude, and preparation of the saints in coming to the meeting. The elders must bear the responsibility to stir up each member of their church to function.* **In order to do this, the elders themselves must have personal contact with the saints. This requires their time and energy, and this is a real sacrifice."**

88. **"In a previous message, I said that a good elder should contact twenty people a week. This may sound like a large number, but actually it is not. You can contact people by telephone at least three times a day. You can call one in the morning, another one at noon, and still another one at night. If you did this seven days a week, twenty-one people could be contacted."**

89. *"In your contact, you should not just inquire about the saints' welfare. Take the opportunity to fellowship with the saints about the Lord's interest on earth, and take time to have a little prayer with them.* **If you contacted twenty saints in this way, after one month you would see a fresh situation in your locality.** *To contact the saints makes a big difference. To be an elder today, the major thing is to contact people, but you must contact them in the new way."*

90. *"I have been speaking concerning the new way, the God-ordained way for the past seven and a half years, but I have not seen much real practice of the new way. Today, everyone welcomes the new way. Thank the Lord for this. But I still beg you all to have a change."*

Oversight of Groups *(excerpts are mainly from Book 11 of Elders' Training, W.L. 1991)*

91. *"I would like to say a word to the elders concerning the going on of the vital groups. The elders should be those who shepherd the flock."*

92. *"They may be one-hundred percent for the vital groups and yet not charge the flock...* **I am concerned that they may not contact the individual sheep to find out how they are doing in the vital groups.** *"*

93. *"The elders must do something to raise up the saints."*

94. *"They are not only the shepherds, but also the "head sheep" at the head of the flock.* **If the head sheep would not take action, the whole flock will be stopped.** *"*

95. *"The elders do not need to rebuke others. They just need to take care of the sheep."*

96. **"Every week they should contact a few saints for fellowship. Such fellowship will stir up the saints to go on."**

97. **"The elders should take some action to supervise, but they may not like to oversee others to find out the real situation."**

98. *"Some of them may be afraid to do this for fear that the saints will be offended. But I assure you that most of the saints want the elders to visit them. Most of the saints love the elders and want to see them and fellowship with them."*

99. *"A certain saint may not like the elders, but the elders should still try to visit him."*

100. *"After two years, he may tell a particular elder, "Probably, you don't know how much help you rendered to me. Without your coming to visit me two years ago, I would not be here. I might be out of the church life."*

101. *"We should do things according to the need of the Lord. The Lord needs a flock; the Lord needs the elders to shepherd the flock."*

102. *"Of course, I noticed that many of the elders are very careful not to offend the saints or make them unhappy. This is good. But if the parents are always so good to the children and do not correct them, the children will be spoiled.* **I am saying this to point out that eventually the perfected saints will be grateful to the elders who care for them properly."**

103. *"I am burdened that all the saints would rise up to take action.* **I am also burdened to see the elders rise up to supervise and shepherd the flock in order to help them go on in the way of the vital groups."**

104. *"If all of us rise up to contact people every day, the Lord will really have a way to gain something. Just contact one or two people each day. If you do not know how to speak, just speak."*

105. *"If you speak, you will learn how to speak. This training should usher in your action. There is no reason or excuse that you would not take action to contact people."*

106. *"The co-workers and elders should learn how to contact individual saints to fellowship with them particularly concerning the group meetings. We need to fellowship with them how to have the mutual teaching, the mutual asking and answering of questions, the mutual*

fellowship, the mutual interceding, the mutual care, and the mutual shepherding."

> *"The elders should spend time to teach each one of the attendants of the group meetings. They need to go to each of the saints homes outside the group meeting. This is why Paul said in Acts 20 that he taught the saints publicly and from house to house and that he admonished each one of them night and day with tears. Paul used both the day and the night. We mostly use our meeting time to contact the saints. We think that as long as we have attended every meeting, we have fulfilled our duty. But that is not the complete fulfilling of our duty. The fulfilling of our duty is also outside the meetings."*

108. *"There is no way to carry out the God-ordained way except by the individual contact with people. What is needed today is for the full-timers, co-workers, and elders to spend their time, energy, and spiritual capacity to take care of people individually.*

A Word of Love

(W. Lee, 1996, excerpts from the book)

109. *"We all must learn to shepherd one another."*

110. *"This does not mean that since I am shepherding you, I do not need your shepherding."*

111. **"We all have defects and shortcomings. Everyone has defects Therefore, we have to humble ourselves to meet God's grace. This strengthens our spirit to visit people and to take care of people regardless of whether they are good or bad. Regardless of what they are, we must go to visit them and keep visiting."**

112. "*...We have no such law forcing us to go out. However, I am trying my best to help the church build up the vital groups with such a shepherding spirit full of love and care for others.*"

113. "*We need to have this kind of love and go to tell all the dormant ones who think that the Lord condemns them that the church does not condemn anyone. Rather, the church wants to see all the dormant ones come back. If they all would come back, I would weep with tears of thanksgiving to the Lord.*"

114. "*The Lord can testify for me that I do not condemn anyone. We have no qualification to condemn anyone. Without the Lord's mercy, we would be the same as the dormant ones. Therefore, we must love them.*"

115. "*It all depends upon love...'love covers all transgressions'.*" (Prov. 10:12).

116. **"*We love people. We love the opposers, and we love the top rebels. I really mean it. We love them and do not hate them. Who am I? I am not qualified to condemn or hate. Am I perfect?*"**

117. "*Even the prophet Isaiah, when he saw the Lord, said, 'Woe is me, for I am finished / For I am a man of unclean lips, / And in the midst of a people of unclean lips I dwell' (Isa. 6:5). Who is clean today? If we criticize people and say something bad about them, we are not clean.*"

> "*And if I have the gift of prophecy, and know all mysteries and all knowledge, and if I have all faith...**but do not have love, I am nothing.**"*

Next page – *Icemen in the Lord's Recovery*

Icemen in The Lord's Recovery

(Minoru Chen, Atlanta Conference - 1998)

Get this burden: the Lord needs to bring in a revival in His recovery, a revival that is only brought in by a prevailing shepherding church life everywhere. Saints, this is what was in the heart of Brother Lee. I hope that there will be a genuine revival among us by our receiving the burden of shepherding. If all the churches receive this teaching to participate in Christ's wonderful shepherding, there will be a big revival. In the recovery, I thought revival would come in some other way, but Brother Lee left us with a clear promise, that **if we receive this burden of shepherding in the recovery across the board, there will be a certain revival.** I believe this is not just a word of men, but a word from the Lord's heart. Saints, don't we want a revival, a revival where there is blessing that we cannot contain, a revival that overwhelms and baffles us? **Don't you think that kind of revival belongs to the Lord's recovery?**

I tell you, right now someone is waiting for your shepherding. It may be a young person, or it may be a backslidden saint, or one sitting in the periphery. It may be one in your family. Dear saints, someone needs shepherding. You may say, didn't you say the Lord is shepherding them. Yes, but the Lord today is moving in the principle of incarnation. Even I say this with reverence to the Lord, there are some things He cannot do. **He wants so desperately to shepherd that weak one, but He can only do so much. If there is not a member of His that would respond to Him, correspond with Him, to pray and to**

20

be filled with the heart of God, that one will stay in that condition for quite a long time. **And, we have seen this among us. We have seen this in the churches.** And, we have seen this in our lives. Think about it, how many times you wish the doorbell would ring. You may say you are just being bad, you are just being naughty, but actually you wish so-and-so would come now. Saints, we need to shepherd. All of God's recovery work by life is in this shepherding. I tell you, our main service in the church is shepherding.

I say again that shepherding is the all-inclusive care that includes two things: the side of cherishing and the side of nourishing. Cherishing is in His humanity; nourishing is in His divinity. Cherishing is just to warm up someone, to make them happy, to make them joyful…By then they would be ready for any message you want to give them. Don't despise cherishing. **I feel, actually, in the Lord's move we are rather short of shepherding. This is why in many places the feeling is cold, the atmosphere is icy, the relationship is distant in many churches. It is not warm, it is not ardent, it is not hot, it is not burning.** Dear saints, don't try to pray and then the Spirit comes down and we will all be hot. Start to care and start to warm up. I don't mean this in a natural way. We have to do this in the humanity of Christ, which is altogether in resurrection and not in the natural man. Nevertheless, Christ in resurrection is not cold. I tell you, some of us think that the ascended Christ must be like a piece of ice, ruling and reigning there. I don't think so. I think today His Manhood is more than ever before. Why? He's become a man! I tell you, He is the warmest Person in the universe. **Saints, let His warmth go as the electrum through you. Let His warmth come out of you!**

You know, I was born an icy person. I still am. Oh, I need help. I really do. Because I found out my icy nature is not suitable for shepherding or for God's recovery work. Too many times, when I see a saint I turn away or pretend not to see them. For people like me, I need to practice hugging. Brother, come up here. I need

to practice hugging. (He hugs the brother.) I don't mean holy hug movement. Please don't do that. **But, surely, the recovery has a lot of icemen that need to practice some hugging.** I know that if it is from the source of God, something is transmitted, passed on of a healing nature, of an encouraging nature. Dear saints, how about let's make all of our church life hot, loving. How about that? You can do it with the love of God. Love prevails. Love prevails. I tell you, to do this kind of shepherding, love is the first thing. Love is everything. In fact, if you read 1 Corinthians 13, love believes, endures, hopes, love is everything. Why? Because in true shepherding, the greatest need is long suffering and patience. That is something I found out. Maybe I'm wrong, but that's what I found out. **Oh, you look at this one and almost you hate him. But you cannot hate him, he is your brother. In fact, you have to shepherd him. Oh, what do you need? You need something you don't have. It's called what? Not just love, but patience, and endurance. Yesterday, I talked to a brother. Oh, I just complained to him about this one. Afterwards, I had to call the brother and say 'brother, I'm sorry'. What kind of shepherd is this?** Oh dear saints, we need the Lord as our long suffering, as our endurance, and as our hope. I tell you, in shepherding the saints you have to be always hopeful. Even the worst situation is hopeful; the most terrible brother, hopeful; the most impossible case, hopeful. Then you can shepherd. Aren't you a hopeless case yourself? Anyway, the burden is, may the Lord recover the spirit and heart of shepherding in His recovery, to bring in a genuine revival that will carry out God's recovery work of life…."

Next page – *Not Through Rebuke or Condemnation*

Not through Rebuke or Condemnation
With Any Kind of Negative Spirit, Attitude, and Tone

Witness Lee shared, "Our gaining of people, however, should not be through rebuke or condemnation with any kind of negative spirit, attitude, and tone. To be a good elder, the first thing one must learn is not to rebuke people. Through many mistakes, we have learned that rebuking never works. For this reason, Paul said, 'And the fathers, do not provoke your children to anger, but nurture them in the discipline and admonition of the Lord' (Eph. 6:4). If we do not rebuke our children when we discipline them, they will not be provoked. Provoking comes from rebuking. If a child misbehaves and we rebuke him, he will be provoked. Instead, we should spend a pleasant time with him, and in this time, we will be able to pass on the proper knowledge of how to behave.

"In I Corinthians, Paul strongly rebuked the believers in Corinth. In doing this, however, he had affliction and anguish of heart (2 Cor. 2:4 For out of much affliction and anguish of heart I wrote to you through many tears, not that you would be made sorrowful, but that you would know the love which I have more abundantly toward you.) Moreover, he had no rest in his spirit until the good news came through Titus telling him of the Corinthians' positive response. (7:6) At that time the great burden in his heart was relieved. This indicates that there was a great danger in Paul's rebuke of the believers. The Lord Jesus at times also strongly rebuked certain people. However, we are not the Lord

Jesus. He surely knows how much to rebuke people and when to do it. We, however, have often rebuked people foolishly. Nothing exposes our foolishness as much as our rebuking. The more we rebuke people the more foolish we are. (Letters 1-6, p. 19) We are one with Christ, but only to a partial degree. We are still too much in the old man, in the natural life. Unconsciously and unintentionally we often do the wrong things together with the right things. Therefore, it is always safer not to rebuke.

"Watchman Nee testified that he received much help from sister M.E. Barber, who rebuked him often. She was very deep in the Lord and had especially learned the lesson of the subjective cross of Christ. She learned the lesson of bearing the cross, and she learned the lesson of praying and of living in the light of the Lord's appearing. However, her shortcoming was in the matter of frankness and rebuking. **Although she was in China for many years, only one person, Watchman Nee, was raised up through her. According to Brother Nee, there were over twenty young people under her care, but eventually nearly all left. Only Brother Nee returned to her to be rebuked.**

"The problems in a church are often related to the elders, and most of the problems related to the elders arise from the elders' negative spirit, attitude, and tone toward others. It is very difficult not to have a negative spirit. Our spirit, attitude, tone, and gesture may all offend people." - Witness Lee, 1991, Elders' Training Book 11, p. 23-26.

Next page – *A Foolish Thought*

A Foolish Thought

In the book, <u>Church Affairs</u>, Watchman Nee talks about the need to care for people who are having problems. His concept was to help people by solving, not avoiding their problems. He said, *"I want the brothers and sisters to know about a foolish thought. I do not know when this thought began. Some people indeed have thought that in the church life we should not encounter problems. But please remember from the time of the apostolic church problems have existed. The church has always been a church of problems and not a church without problems....Many foolish brothers think that being free from problems is a sign that a church is spiritual. But please keep in mind that the sign of a church being spiritual is not that it is free from problems. Instead, the sign of a church being spiritual depends upon whether it has ways to solve problems and whether those ways are appropriate. Once a church becomes spiritual, many problems will have to be considered. If a church is not spiritual, it is peaceful and without problems. The more spiritual you are, the more problems you have to solve"* (p. 48, 151).

In a section called *Caring For Problems,* Brother Nee suggests that certain weightier brothers and sisters take care of those *"encountering hardship"* and those having *"difficulties and conflicts in the family"* and *"pray for them"* and *"solve the problems"* they are having. He said, **"Whenever brothers and sisters hear that something has happened among some brothers and sisters, they need to notify immediately these brothers** and sisters [the caring ones] and allow them to find a way to meet the need."

Watchman Nee had a definite approach in mind of helping the saints with their problems and not ignoring the needs in the Body (p. 47).

Concerning asking for help and being open with others he said, as was shared earlier, *"Brothers, if you do not learn how to bear the burdens of others, and if you do not seek out the help from others regarding your own burdens, you do not know what the Body is, nor can you have coordination in the work…If we stay in our former condition, we are still tightly wrapped in ourselves…Then my affairs are still my affairs, and I will not let you touch them. He told leading ones, "when problems come, you have never once sought someone saying 'I need help'. We need to be an open person… Toward your brother your spirit needs to be open, your thinking needs to be open, and many times your mouth needs to be opened. I hope there will be those among us who can say to the brothers and sisters, 'I have had trouble with this one matter for many years. Please help me overcome it.' If this is the first time in your life that you ask for help, let it be here [on the mountain]"* (p. 179-181).

www.ingramcontent.com/pod-product-compliance
Lightning Source LLC
Chambersburg PA
CBHW051252120626
46547CB00014B/1905